THE SOUND OF MY HEART

COLLECTION OF POEMS

DIPPANITA ROY

Copyright © Dippanita Roy
All Rights Reserved.

ISBN 979-888591055-2

This book has been published with all efforts taken to make the material error-free after the consent of the author. However, the author and the publisher do not assume and hereby disclaim any liability to any party for any loss, damage, or disruption caused by errors or omissions, whether such errors or omissions result from negligence, accident, or any other cause.

While every effort has been made to avoid any mistake or omission, this publication is being sold on the condition and understanding that neither the author nor the publishers or printers would be liable in any manner to any person by reason of any mistake or omission in this publication or for any action taken or omitted to be taken or advice rendered or accepted on the basis of this work. For any defect in printing or binding the publishers will be liable only to replace the defective copy by another copy of this work then available.

Contents

About The Author

Dippanita Roy

Dipannita Roy was born in 1988 in Kolkata, West Bengal. The Sound of My Heart is her first book of a romantic poetry collection where she expressed inner romantic feelings in her own life. She is co- author of, Echoes of Hope, The Great Indian Anthology, Purely Platonic and many more. One of her heart touching romantic poetry 'Midnight Essence' was published in the book Euphoria by Lemonpeelpress in Edinburg, Scotland UK. She holds a double masters degree in English and Environment. She did her diploma in Neuro Linguistic Programming from American Board of Neuro Linguistic Programming. She has experience in the financial and automotive industry. Dipannita is a social activist. For five years she has been working with street children. She is an influencer and motivational speaker. She was awarded the ZIIEI Teacher Innovation Award.

When she is not writing, Dipannita spends most of her time reading, cooking and playing piano. She is a blogger, traveller. Love to spend time with family and friends.

About The Book

'The Sound Of My Heart' is a romantic poetry collection, where the author conveys her inner feelings on love in her life. She feels happiness, hate and betrayal in love and inspires to pen down her feelings on paper. In each poetry she stitches words with the essence of love and sorrow which gives the reader a warm heart melting touch. She believes this is not just a book, heart of unsaid feelings.

One Moonlight Night

Sitting in a gracy moonlight night
Hands on hand
Gazing in your eyes.
My restless body,
Calm down slowly......slowly
With glory.
I realise, we are one
No one can separate us,
We remove all spun.
See, today those stars,
This universe
Are dancing, celebrating our love
Promise me, you are mine forever.

Dipannita Roy

CHAPTER TWO

Ray of Love

Sun going to be set
Behind the evening clouds,
The last ray of the day
Hover over your ship deck.
Standing together,
Cuddling each other,
Playing your finger
On my bare neck.
I love to see myself,
In your charming eyes
Where all world going
To be lost.
Darken evening,
Saying something
Find me, under the blanket
Of the sky.

Dipannita Roy

CHAPTER THREE

Second Dream

A faded letter,
Come to my hand in breezing
Soliloquy lady gazing,
Her deep eyes saying
Something
To her lover.
Would you be mine forever.
Stars light flickered.....
In your eyebrows,
Beseeded pain smashed in frost
When your heartfelt dream,
Come to my life.....
My dyeing life will get
A divine vibes.

Dipannita Roy

CHAPTER FOUR

Shredded Doll

Faded sky surpassing
Over my head,
Yellow cool breeze
Surprising me
To come in my doorstep,
Fostering shredded doll,
going to frazzle my heart,
Would you like to see
Ruin me like that.
Am not a piece of show,
Not a robotic pie
Feelings are going to
Shuttered, in flaunt.....
Am going to die,
Scorching clothes are now,
Floating blooded water.
Fumes spreading,
Burning body is there.

Dipannita Roy

CHAPTER FIVE

Last Word

Understanding between us,
Never ending
Long journey, we are going.
Frozen heart thinking,
Reflection of your last word
That you did a sin.
Darkened sight,
Beside this night
Am fighting with my mind,
Fading moon light
Unable to captivate my heart
Without you,
Mine earth is bare apart.

Dipannita Roy

CHAPTER SIX

Tears In Heaven

With the rising sun,
A bouquet of red rose
Fallen from the sky.
A mysterious smile,
With heavenly shy.....

Dear,,, my death is coming near,
Waiting for long to see you,
It is a burden for me.
Give me thy heavenly peace.
Where white cloud floating
With honey bees.
Am seeing, your heavenly tears
Welcome me,
Full of glee.

D. Roy

Divine Love

Waves of Joy

Those delightful waves,
Coming on the sea- shore
Floating sand dunes
Rolling on.
Salted water washed away
Our feet.
We are staring
To go wipe the ship.

We sung a song
Of joyfulness.
We passed many years
Of togetherness.
We experienced hard times,
Like strong waves.
There is nothing without you,
Without sand in waves.

D. Roy

CHAPTER NINE

Shadow

Rain come down
Her footsteps, forlorn my heart
Am gasping in her dark scarf
Shadowy window panes,,
Reflected in her bloody eyes,,
Grisly cold hand
Scribble on paper.
She is in pain,
Her beloved redolence
Make her insane.
Cold, soothing air
Passed her wetted hair,,
Touch my teary face.
Every beat of my heart,,
Shut, for a moment.
Thundering storm
Wrecking outside again.

D. Roy

CHAPTER TEN

Waiting for her marriage Day

She is stitching her,,,,
White lace gown.....
Studded stone shining
Welcoming her marriage day.
Sitting in front of mirror,,
Moving her finger
Remembering, beloved mate.
She is smiling,
Shying
Talking with herself.
Hearing sometimes.....
Her lover footsteps.
Soft roses petals,,,
Singing, dancing with joy.
Embalming her beauty.....
With love,,,
Not for herself,,,
Only for her beloved.

D. Roy

CHAPTER ELEVEN

Evening Shade

Lantern bulb sparkling in...
Dusky sky
Some are fallen
Some are nearby.
Your precious smile
Precious like child,,
We swinging together,,,
Any sea-beach side.
Our spiritual closeness,,
Love profoundly sprouted
Dazzling stars
Piled on my eyelashes.
Warmth evening,
Kisses cold waves....
Our blazing heart
Mesmerise in their way.

D. Roy

Rest of My life thinking you

Unlock the door
Where soothing breeze
Capitulate near me.
Flowing slender hair,
Remembering those days
When you touch my shining face.
Purple tree,
Remembering those days
Lying together, under the branches.
There is way,,
Bank of the river
Our feet in white foam.
Curious sand asking our destiny,
Don't know where to go.

D. Roy

Someday With You

Soft strings of my heart
Produces melody
With your warmness.
Nothing is empty here,
When am with you
Today crystal sky
Turned blue.
Soul getting lost,
In your intrepid shadow,,,,
My bare hands get now,,,
A brave hand
Where i concede
Rest of my life.

D. Roy

CHAPTER FOURTEEN

Eyes Mirror

You are looking erotic
When water droplet cruise
On your buttery skin.
My finger moving,,
Your deep navel point
Smudging my lips
Melt my heart.
With a warm kiss,
I can see myself
In your magical eyes,,
Tonight.
Moving your dishevelled hair,,
From your bare neck,
And squeezing you in
My arms.
This night, i see
My love in your eyes
When you moaning my name
Feeling your body pain.
How can i moved my,
Naked arms.
Hugging your restless body
Kissing your palms.

D. Roy

CHAPTER FIFTEEN

Timmy's Eloquent Smile

Flowers blooming,
Like an innocent child
No one can define
How sensitive smile
You have.
Galaxies make
Their way.
When your divine step
Firm newborn stars.
Timmy.....your one smile
Gives me
Soothing touch.....
You don't know
I like this so much.
Behind this smile,
You told me a lot
In my paradise
With you
No gain, and no loss.

D. Roy

CHAPTER SIXTEEN

The Last Petal

Sensuous fragrance
Of lily
Coming from your wrist.
We are sitting close,
So close
Hearing each other
Pulse beat.
I kiss on your wrist,
Yes, not your lips
Not your uncovered skin
Drunken all your
Savour
No lust, felt in my
Heart.
Falling of your last pulse
When i heard
Rhythm of my life
Lost forever.

D. Roy

CHAPTER SEVENTEEN

Our Forgotten Story

There is a mysterious
Heart....inside of you.
My unsolved prediction
Failed to
Read,, i saw
Your diminish glory
Trying to hide
Our forgotten love story.
We met unexpectedly
Do you remember those days,,
Dazzling evening.....
Pampering us so many
Ways.
We failed, we stand
Then,, how this
Solitary days come.
D. Roy

CHAPTER EIGHTEEN

Autumn

Next to my door,
Still you are standing on
Wooden floor.
Still you are looking
For your love,
Someone, someday
Will come
Then autumn craving
Your soul, every drops
Of your thoughts.

Golden leaves never
Goes back with you,
Mine broken gleams
Conceal in gritty heart
Of yours.
Stay away from me,,,,
Where you now
New autumn will come
Another way.......in my door.

D. Roy

Broken Heart

Warm clouds melting
When sun kisses your cheeks,
Your bare shoulder taken rest
Bequeath everything,
Closing eyes deep lashes
Want to fall asleep.
Starting your moist
Forehead
Mine thoughts going to be
Erotic.
You didn't spell a word
Didn't give me a chance,,
To rectify mine fault
To share mine unveil thoughts
Near you.

D. Roy

CHAPTER TWENTY

In A Last Winter Cherry Garden

Snowy december came
With the passionate
Fascination of love.
In the garden full of
Yellow leaves.
The lips of the beauty
More arrogant with
Winter cherry.
She was a lovely lass
Warmness of her dark
Eyebrows,
Melt my stony heart.
Cane basket in her hand
Was busy to work
With full passion.
Seen mesmerise beauty
Of her face,,
When her scarf slipped off
On her face.
Lustrous golden hair
Shining hay.

Went to stop her,
But she scared, shy
Her pinkish cheek blush,
A red velvet flower
Fallen from her basket
In my lap.

D. Roy

Fairy Garden

Snowy moonlight
Come tonight,,,,,
In your fairy garden
It Looks like heaven.
Magic wand when
Touching my sword
Pink petals fallen
On the floor.
Behind from my
Poppies tree
Woven wings fairy
Came down on
Material earth,
Soft- white elegance of pearls.
Would you ever see
The star wand
Touch my feet
Fairy- angels are
Now with me.

D. Roy

In Sojourn Oasis

Thorny valiant sand
Are more dry,
Rough edges, slid
Finger tips.
Your grey hair
Wrinkle pale face
Snatch your
Utmost beauty.
You are growing old age
Slowly vision fade,,
Shrivelled hand
Trembling now.
yOur blank eyes ,,,
Now waiting for death
Nobody come ,,,,to rescue
From your fate.

D. Roy

www.ingramcontent.com/pod-product-compliance
Lightning Source LLC
Chambersburg PA
CBHW070327160726
47999CB00003B/1198